ANY EXCUSE!

HOW TO GET OUT OF DOING ABSOLUTELY EVERYTHING JEM BROWN

Illustrations by Naomi Tipping

summersdale

ANY EXCUSE!

Illustrations by Naomi Tipping

Text contributed by Anna Martin

Summersdale Publishers Ltd
46 West Street
Chichester
West Sussex
PO19 1RP
UK

www.summersdale.com

Printed and bound in Great Britain

ISBN: 978-1-84953-095-8

Substantial discounts on bulk quantities of Summersdale books are available to corporations, professional associations and other organisations. For details contact Summersdale Publishers by telephone: +44 (0) 1243 771107, fax: +44 (0) 1243 786300 or email: nicky@summersdale.com.

CONTENTS

Introduction   5

How to get out of...

... going to work   7

... going to the office party   23

... attending weddings (even your own)   31

... going on a date   41

... Christmas   53

... seeing relatives   60

... taking the dog for a walk   68

... washing the car   74

... general housework   80

... meeting the in-laws   87

... taking the rubbish out   93

... paying the bill   99

... tricky situations involving the police   107

... situations you've never even considered!   116

INTRODUCTION

When crafting the perfect excuse for any given situation, you must approach it in the manner of an Olympic athlete preparing for the race of your life: eat raw eggs, see your body as a machine, wear trainers with go-faster stripes... Thinking on your feet is a skill that takes years to hone. That sounds too much like hard work, doesn't it? Well, for all you armchair Olympians out there it's lucky that you've picked up this book! Think no more, as you now have the best excuses for any given situation at your fingertips, all in one handy pocket-sized package.

So the next time you're asked 'Would you take the dog for a walk, dear?' as you've settled in for an evening of telly with a takeaway perched on your knees, just whip out this little marvel of a book and find a fail-safe response to get out of it!

I nearly **choked** to death on my filling when eating one of those cheap toffees you gave me at work. I need some recovery time – at least a week.

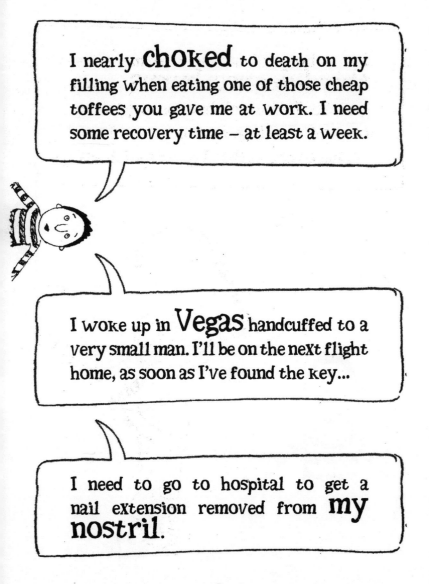

I woke up in **Vegas** handcuffed to a very small man. I'll be on the next flight home, as soon as I've found the key...

I need to go to hospital to get a nail extension removed from **my nostril**.

I am currently under attack from a rather inclement reaction to either the roast vegetables from yesterday or porridge this morning, which is rendering me incapable of human interaction... without causing some kind of **olfactory offence!**

I woke up with 15 **traffic cones** in my bed this morning, which is really odd because I went to bed at ten with a cup of cocoa. I can barely move!

My house has fallen down a **hole** – turns out it was built on an old mine shaft. The emergency services are trying to extract me from the rubble. I'll keep you posted on my progress.

I'm down to my last pound after playing **bingo online** for most of the night, so I don't have enough money left for the train to work. Don't worry – I'll try to win some cash back today while I'm off.

I had a particularly energetic game of *Twister* last night and I've done my back in – these company dos get out of hand, don't they?

I can't come in today, the springs on the **garage door** have broken and I can't get the car out.

My wife is planning to **conceive** today and I'd like to be there when it happens.

I'm having a **staring** competition with my housemate, if I lose I'll have to give him my job. His lids are twitching so I'm hoping...

Sorry, I won't be in for the next fortnight. I went to see my sister off on her **cruise** but the ship sailed off with me still on it. The captain refused to turn back, so it looks like I'll be stuck in the **Bahamas** for the next few weeks.

I have to know whether Sheila and Hank survived the **accident** in *The People That Live Next Door*. I've had a sleepless night worrying about them, poor loves.

I think my new **satnav** must be faulty – I took a wrong turn. I think I'm somewhere near Oban.

I'm too **fat** to get into my work overalls. I put on ten kilos over the weekend because of the stress.

I dislodged a **wasps' nest** whilst gardening at the weekend. I've been on the run ever since. They just won't stop chasing me.

My **dog** has buried one of my work shoes and my favourite work pen in the garden. I'm just digging up the place to try and find it.

Sorry for being late, because of the **pay freeze** I had to pawn my alarm clock yesterday.

After my recent trip **Down Under**, I decided to set all the clocks to Australian time to help me stay in the holiday mood. I came into work on Sunday, so didn't think you'd mind me having Friday off instead.

I'm at the **golf course** with Mr Hawasaki, you know, our Japanese contact that you told me to spend some time with?

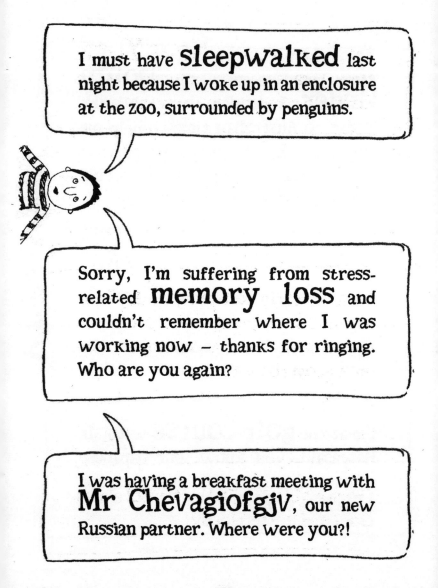

I must have **sleepwalked** last night because I woke up in an enclosure at the zoo, surrounded by penguins.

Sorry, I'm suffering from stress-related **memory loss** and couldn't remember where I was working now – thanks for ringing. Who are you again?

I was having a breakfast meeting with **Mr Chevagiofgjv**, our new Russian partner. Where were you?!

I thought we ran on **New York** time because we're owned by an American company now, my mistake!

I was up early collecting **slugs** for my son's school project and got bitten by an adder. I'm just waiting for the antivenom to kick in.

I have a **solar-powered** alarm clock and it was cloudy.

I **smell** really bad this morning and am in dire need of a bath — except I can't find the plug.

Excuse for being late: I worked **twice as fast** yesterday afternoon, so I figured that you wouldn't mind me missing work this morning.

I decided to have a **barbecue** for breakfast this morning and I'm still waiting for the chicken to cook through. You wouldn't want me getting salmonella, would you?

Excuse for being late: I'm just reading the **staff handbook** you gave me. I got completely absorbed and forgot the time.

I really wish I could be at the party but my friend might be going on *Who Wants to be a Millionaire?* and I'm her **phone a friend**. I can't risk missing the call.

My **astrology** reading says any social interaction with colleagues today could lead to romance, which worries me because they're all married. I don't want to cause any marital strife.

The last time I went for work drinks I ended up on the table doing the cancan and I **kicked my boss** in the face. It's taken me a good nine months to get back into his good books, so I can't risk any more mishaps.

I was once queuing up at a **buffet** and had reached the front, when an eagle swooped down and snatched the food right from my plate. I've been traumatised ever since and can't go near a buffet for fear of the eagle.

I wouldn't want to show everyone up with my amazing **dance moves**.

I bought a new dress especially for the party but when I got home yesterday my **cat** had completely **shredded** it. In fact, she had shredded everything in my wardrobe. So you see I have absolutely nothing to wear.

I just know there are going to be **sausage rolls**, and I've been clean for two months now. I wouldn't want to undo all my hard work.

I'd better not. I'm a bit of a liability at social functions. After a few drinks I get this sense of clarity that makes me tell people **exactly what I think** of them.

I **twisted** my ankle running away from next door's dog this morning. I need to rest it.

I still haven't got over last year's embarrassment with the whole **stapler incident**.

After Phil from accounts declared his **undying love** for me at last year's party I think it would be too awkward. Especially as he still sends me flowers once a week.

My **twin** is banned from all the drinking establishments in town and I have great difficulty in convincing them that I'm not him. I wouldn't want to cause a scene.

I've got to go home and sew name-tapes into my partner's **pants**.

I saw the **weather** report this morning and it looked so bad that I assumed you would be postponing it.

Oh, I thought the wedding invite was a **joke** – it arrived on 1 April, you see.

You know the train on your dress? Well, I **blew my nose** on it at your last fitting – it was the first thing to hand and I couldn't resist.

But I was there! I thought you looked different – much **hairier** than I remembered and that piercing on your left nipple certainly wasn't there before!

I'm not sure if I should come. I don't think I'll be able to keep it a secret that you bought her engagement ring from **Argos**.

My car broke down outshide a **pub** sooo I went in and had a few little drinkies while waiting for the nice AA man and now I'm tooooo **drunk** to even walk to the venue, ssssorry!

Sorry, who are you again? I don't remember you from **school** – are you sure you've got the right person?

I've borrowed a **golf cart** to get to the wedding – my car broke down next to a golf course. I'll be there in about five hours.

I was so embarrassed about clashing with the **bridesmaids** that I dashed home to get changed, but I couldn't find a thing to wear!

I'm all wedding'd-out, sorry. What with that one on *EastEnders* the other night, then that one on *Corrie* – it's too much!

I don't know where I am, but when I find out I'll let you know so you can come and pick me up! Oh, and please bring me some **clothes!** [Only works on the morning after a stag do.]

I'm up to my knees in **shit**! There's sewage pouring into my basement. I'll be there as soon as it's cleared!

I heard a rumour that *OK!* are going to be doing a 24-page story on the wedding and I've just got the most almighty spot on my forehead. I couldn't possibly be photographed for a national magazine; it would be social suicide!

I was the chimney sweep in the **graveyard** to bring you luck – it's my new job. Didn't you notice me?

I'll only come if you let me do my **death metal** version of 'D-I-V-O-R-C-E'!

I was watching *Phone Booth* last night and I'm too scared to put the receiver down!

I got the wedding list through and I'm still saving up for the designer **toaster**. I was too embarrassed to come without a present.

I went to your first wedding and look what happened to that one. I thought I might be a **bad omen**.

I have this thing about **wedding cakes**. I see one and I just want to dive on it.

Thanks for picking me as **best man**, I've got a telegram to read. Apparently it's from a girl called Tina who you met that time in Vegas? You know, the one you met at the casino and married on a whim after winning the jackpot on the slot machines. Oh wait, just looking at it, I think it's a request for maintenance payments for the twins she's just had. That'll bring the house down!

I'm **allergic** to flowers, royal icing, lace, cummerbunds, top hats, vicars, stupid handwritten place-settings, vows, distant relatives, doilies and especially bridesmaids!

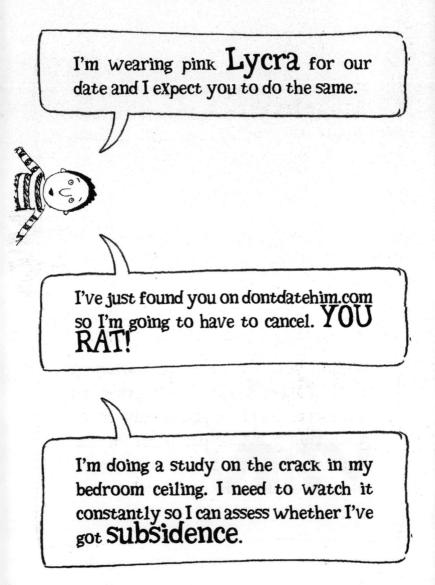

I'm wearing pink **Lycra** for our date and I expect you to do the same.

I've just found you on dontdatehim.com so I'm going to have to cancel. YOU RAT!

I'm doing a study on the crack in my bedroom ceiling. I need to watch it constantly so I can assess whether I've got **subsidence**.

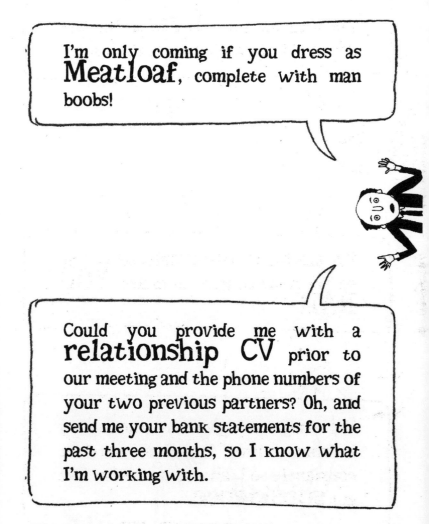

I'm only coming if you dress as **Meatloaf**, complete with man boobs!

Could you provide me with a **relationship CV** prior to our meeting and the phone numbers of your two previous partners? Oh, and send me your bank statements for the past three months, so I know what I'm working with.

Yeah, you know on my profile I put 'a bit **scatty**'? Well, I forgot I was meeting you so I've double-booked myself.

I bet my friend that I could stay in the bath for a week. I've been in here for four days so far, but I'm getting quite **wrinkly**.

My **glass eye** fell out and rolled under the washing machine. It might take me a while to find it, but I'll be there when I can!

My **terrapin** died, and as I flushed it down the toilet the cistern broke and my bathroom flooded. As I went outside to get my neighbour, who's a plumber, I accidentally locked myself out. I tried to climb back in through the window, but I caught my dressing gown on the window and I fell naked to the ground. I'm traumatised and can't possibly come out for the next few days.

I'm afraid I can't come out tonight because my **moon** is in Aquarius and yours is in Gemini – it would be a disaster.

46

I can't go out with you because my **gay** lover, who is about to go to jail, is actually straight and is cheating on me with my sister, whose husband I had an affair with two months ago.

I need to take a picture of the *Flying Scotsman* tonight – it's hardly ever in this area and it's one I haven't got in my **trainspotting** manual.

I'm reading *Twilight* and I've just got to the good bit.

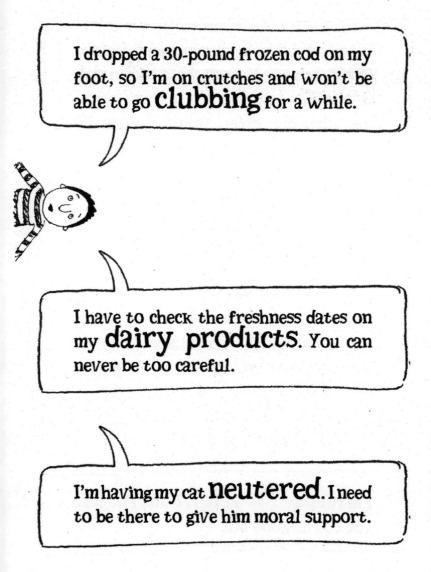

I dropped a 30-pound frozen cod on my foot, so I'm on crutches and won't be able to go **clubbing** for a while.

I have to check the freshness dates on my **dairy products**. You can never be too careful.

I'm having my cat **neutered**. I need to be there to give him moral support.

I need to count the bristles on my **toothbrush**. The packet says it has even more bristles than the last one. I need to make sure, and if it hasn't, get my money back.

My dad's got to go to the **football**, and I never go on dates without him.

I need to sit in a darkened room and think about **world issues**.

I won't be able to see you for at least three months – not while *Doctor Who* series 110 is running.

Sorry, but I've just remembered when I met you at speed dating that you said you hated **Kylie**. To me that's sacrilege – I can't possibly meet up with you now.

I've got crabs!

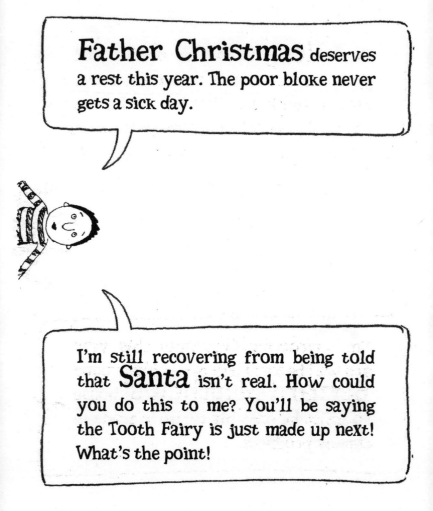

Father Christmas deserves a rest this year. The poor bloke never gets a sick day.

I'm still recovering from being told that **Santa** isn't real. How could you do this to me? You'll be saying the Tooth Fairy is just made up next! What's the point!

I'm **allergic** to pine needles and your mother insists on having a live tree in the house. It's her fault, she obviously doesn't want me there.

I'm boycotting Christmas this year and will be forming a picket line around **Bernard Matthews'** house to insist he ends his barbaric trade in turkey products.

I've been too **naughty** this year.

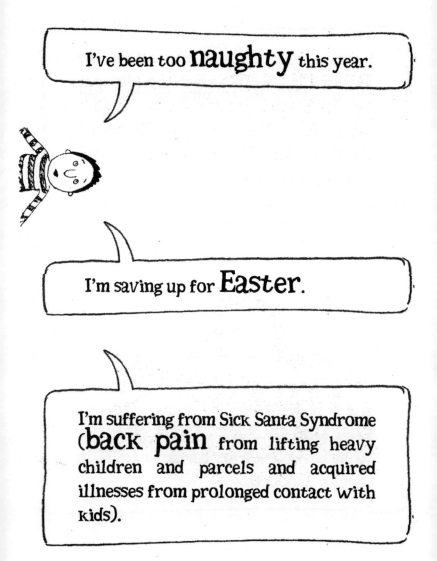

I'm saving up for **Easter**.

I'm suffering from Sick Santa Syndrome (**back pain** from lifting heavy children and parcels and acquired illnesses from prolonged contact with kids).

I can't make it this year – I've won *The X Factor*! Didn't you see me on the telly? I've got loads of promos to do. I won't be free until at least next Christmas – when my album is in the bargain bucket.

I've become a Jehovah's Witness. Can I tell you all about the good news?

But my parents told me it was only every **leap year**?

Can I pick the film this year for the whole family? It's gotta be *Fight Club*!

You know how my dad loves **Jamaican rum**? I thought I'd go that extra mile this year and buy it *in* Jamaica for him. Unfortunately, the only flight I could get was on Christmas Eve, so I'll see you in the New Year.

I'm doing a **colonic detox** at the moment so I can't come to the family meal, unless you have an industrial supply of toilet paper at the ready, and it needs to be floral.

I fell asleep when I was sunbathing at the beach yesterday. All I can do is walk around naked and apply **after-sun**.

I'm sorry, but I can't help but stare at the enormous **mole** between your mother's eyebrows – it makes me quite queasy.

My recent course of **Botox** has left me looking like the Bride of Wildenstein. I wouldn't want to scare the children.

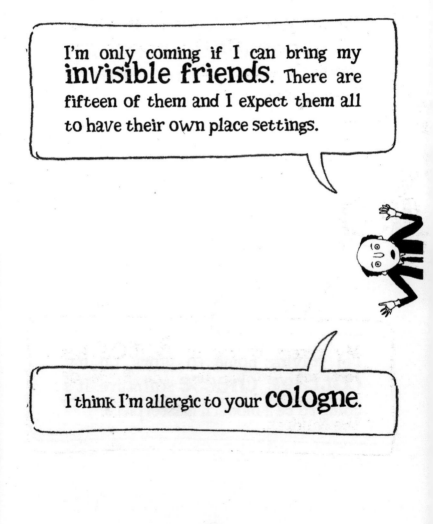

I'm only coming if I can bring my **invisible friends**. There are fifteen of them and I expect them all to have their own place settings.

I think I'm allergic to your **cologne**.

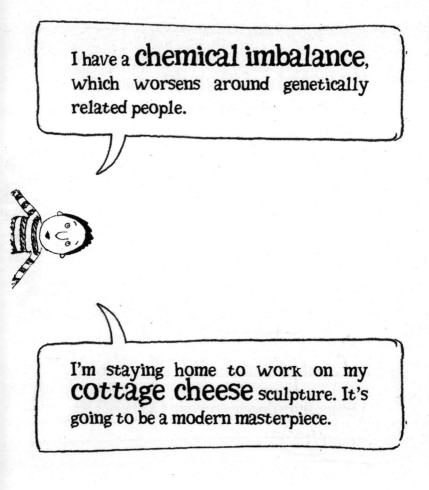

I have a **chemical imbalance**, which worsens around genetically related people.

I'm staying home to work on my **cottage cheese** sculpture. It's going to be a modern masterpiece.

You know, the more time I spend around my family, the more I'm convinced that I'm a child of **Satan**.

I don't think it's a good idea for the family to get together unless it's on *The Jeremy Kyle Show*. I think I'll make enquiries to see if they have space for us and you can invite them.

But Aunty Jane always insists on knitting me something and making me wear it for the whole day. Last time she gave me some crochet dungarees and the **chafing** was appalling — I had to take two weeks off work and lie in a hammock covered in Savlon.

I've just taken three **Viagra** by mistake. I don't think I have any trousers baggy enough to avoid extreme embarrassment.

You mean they're still alive? Whose **funeral** was it that we went to six months ago? I'm pretty sure it was theirs, certain in fact.

HOW TO GET OUT OF...

... TAKING THE DOG FOR A WALK

These **shoes** are new and I'm breaking them in. I can only walk around inside.

I only walk backwards in a north-easterly direction. I need to be facing the **Sirius star** at all times in order to benefit from its healing properties.

It's against my **religious beliefs** to walk the dog. Animals should be free to roam wherever they want.

I'm just on the brink of finishing my great first **novel** that will turn our lives around!

I feel a **cold** coming on. I'd best not go out just in case, or I'll end up missing dinner with your family tomorrow.

Last time I took your dog for a walk, loads of women tried to **chat me up**. I managed to resist them last time, but only just.

I didn't want to tell you, but I **lost** your dog last time I took him for a walk. I **found** him about an hour later playing with four identical dogs – I just did 'Ip, Dip, Sky, Blue' to choose one to bring back home.

Your dog hates me, as soon as you're out of sight he starts bullying me – please don't make me go!

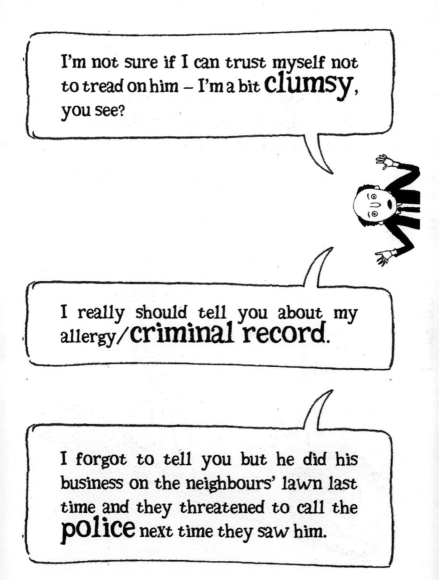

I'm not sure if I can trust myself not to tread on him – I'm a bit **clumsy**, you see?

I really should tell you about my allergy/**criminal record**.

I forgot to tell you but he did his business on the neighbours' lawn last time and they threatened to call the **police** next time they saw him.

I'm afraid of **sponges** – my brother told me they have hidden teeth. I can't even look at a sponge. Please don't make me.

Traffic officers are always drawn to clean **shiny cars**. By not washing the car I'm actually helping you avoid any unwanted attention from the police.

In some **cultures** it's a sign of high status to have a dirty car.

That **squirrel** over there gave me a funny look. I'm too scared to be outside alone with it. I've heard stories of squirrels scratching people's eyes out – especially when near **soapy water**.

Nobody would want to **steal** a dirty car. Therefore I think we should never wash it again.

It looks like it might **snow**. I wouldn't want the car to freeze over. As soon as the sun comes out I'll go and wash it.

I heard that **lightning** is more likely to strike clean cars than dirty ones.

I had a dream I'm going to win the **lottery** some time soon. There's no point washing the car because I'll just buy us a new clean one when I win.

If I wash the car I won't recognise it and will have no chance of finding it in a **busy car park**.

Is it **my turn** again? It can't be! I need photographic and written evidence before I will even consider it!

I don't want people **staring at you.**

I heard on the radio that there's a **water shortage.**

Hoovering is akin to sucking out the **SOUl** of the carpet. I read somewhere that carpets have feelings too, especially ones with patterns.

It's now been scientifically proven that dust is **good for you**.

I'm trying to cultivate the right conditions to grow mould for **biology** experiments.

I've decided to adopt an **eco-friendly** way of life. There are too many chemicals in cleaning products. From now on I hope you can respect my new beliefs and never ask me to clean again. Ever.

I think creased T-shirts are really **sexy**.

I'm trying out the eclectic look. All the celebrities are doing it in their homes. Yes it's supposed to look messy, that's the whole idea, it's called **messy chic**.

If we leave it long enough, **Kim** and **Aggie** will turn up at the door. I've applied to be on the programme.

I'm reading *Charlotte's Web* and I really can't tidy in case I too have a friendly talking **spider** living in my room.

I'm too upset to do the washing up. My **goldfish** died last week and that piece of carrot floating in there just made me think of him.

Sorry, you want me to iron your clothes? I don't own an iron – all my clothes are drip-dry **polyester**.

I actually already cleaned my room, but **the cat** made it messy again. Honestly, I left the room for ten minutes and this is what I came back to.

The last time I changed the bed, I got **lost** in the duvet cover for hours and found another world in there – only it wasn't like **Narnia**, it was a world of despair, where everyone drank cabbage beer and had terrible wind – the smell was awful. I'd rather not go back there.

Did I tell you I have **Tourette's**? But only around parents – it's a very rare form.

Don't you know it's **bad luck** to meet your future in-laws before you get married? I'm pretty sure its bad luck after the wedding as well, but I'll check that one out.

Ooh, I could teach them how to **lap dance**. I must wash my tassels in time!

You know how your dad always wears a **tweed jacket**? I can't be in the same room as tweed. Even if he doesn't wear the tweed jacket, just knowing that he has previously worn tweed is enough. I wouldn't be able to sleep for months.

I've decided to attempt an around-the-world **balloon trip**. I'm not sure when I'll be back – definitely not in time for Sunday dinner.

I would love to meet your parents but I said I'd help Pete milk his **COW** today.

Parents don't like me! No, really, it's a bad idea. The last time I met someone's parents I **projectile vomited** through their letterbox – I couldn't help myself. I then dropped my trousers and sang 'Happy Birthday, Mr President' while perched on their priceless Chippendale sideboard before French-kissing their koi carp. I didn't even know I did any of these things – my ex had to tell me about it because I woke up on the floor of a Hovercraft destined for Jersey 15 hours later.

I think I may have met your mother before, through a **dating** website. I wasn't going to tell you, but I think now is the time to bring it up. I'm not sure if I could keep it from your dad, and I've heard he has a very fine gun collection.

After meeting Dave at the pub last night, things got a bit out of hand. I've now got some unfortunate writing in permanent marker across my **forehead**. Words that I don't think your parents would want to see.

But my friends are **rubbish**! Look, here's John, the empty milk carton, I've had him for six months now, and here's Patsy, my apple core, isn't she pretty?

I couldn't possibly do that — I've been terrified that something or someone lives in the bin ever since I saw that freaky character that lives in a bin on *Sesame Street* when I was really young.

I'm allergic to those wheelie bins – I think it's the type of plastic that they're made of. It makes me come out in **hives**.

I can't deny you that job, dear. It's an excuse for a bit of **fresh air** and you're always saying you don't get enough **exercise**!

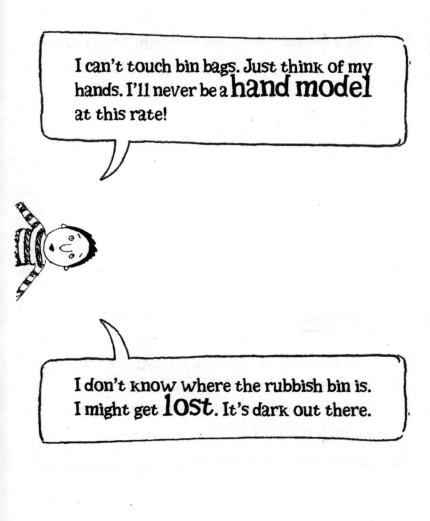

I can't touch bin bags. Just think of my hands. I'll never be a **hand model** at this rate!

I don't know where the rubbish bin is. I might get **lost**. It's dark out there.

My spirit guide is strongly advising me against taking the rubbish out – it will disturb the sensitive chakra energy in my solar plexus and may cause negative impulses that will interfere with my **cosmic order**.

These **nail** extensions cost me £200 – it would be literally throwing money away if I lost one of these tips.

Let's **arm wrestle** and the person that loses can pay. I'm just going to nominate that 25-stone man over there to take my place though – I can't be seen doing something so unladylike in public.

Someone **stole** my credit cards, my cheque book and my savings book, oh, and my purse! Sorry.

You mean the currency isn't **shells** round here? I've got plenty of those!

What? I thought it was **on the house**. I've never paid in here before.

My children have just learned how to use **pinking shears** and they got a bit happy with my pockets, sorry guys! I must invest in one of those man bags.

I'm like the queen; I don't carry **currency** of any kind.

I don't believe in **going Dutch** – what does that mean anyway? Wearing clogs and smoking wacky substances? That's not for me, no.

Oh, was that a bill you sent me? I thought it was some new kind of **sudoku** puzzle. I'm rubbish at those things so I chucked it in the bin.

Now, I don't want to cause a scene but my **ex-boyfriend** is over there – no, don't look round – and he said that if he ever saw me again he would chase me out of town. I'll wait in the car while you settle up.

It is my birthday in three months. Let's call it an **early present.**

My boyfriend has left me and just looking at bills makes me think of all the great times we shared. It makes each one special so I keep them safe under my pillow. I couldn't possibly pay them and send them back; it would send me **over the edge**!

I made some lovely festive paper chains with that **red letter** you sent me – so kind of you to think of me at Christmas.

HOW TO GET OUT OF...

...TRICKY SITUATIONS
INVOLVING THE POLICE

Sorry officer, I saw the flashing lights but I thought you were after the person in front of me so I **sped up** to try and get out of the way.

Derren Brown made me do it.

My **ferret** got loose in the car and he was working his way up my trouser leg. It's very difficult to drive in a straight line with a ferret up your trousers, sir!

I can't help **swerving** when I drive, officer. It's the front end of my car, it always does that.

I dropped a **cigarette** in my lap, and when I was trying to put it out I inadvertently pushed down on the accelerator.

Sorry officer, I know I was speeding. But I was trying to catch up to that red Ford to tell them that their **indicators** aren't working.

I just pulled out of the car wash. I must have slipped on the **soap**.

My air conditioning is broken and I was trying to fight off **heat exhaustion** by driving fast to make a breeze.

I'm sorry officer but without my **glasses** I can't see the speedometer.

My **contact lens** fell out and I was trying to put it back in. I needed both hands, so I didn't have a spare one for the steering wheel.

My friend called and said he just saw my wife **cheating** on me. I've got to get back to the house before the guy leaves.

I wasn't driving **straight** because your headlights were obscuring my view of the road.

I didn't know I was speeding, I must have **nodded off**.

I had to eat these crab sticks. I'm **pregnant**, you see, and it's a craving of mine. I needed both hands.

It's this dance music on the **radio** – it makes me drive too fast! I think it should be banned.

I'm not drunk, officer. I was demonstrating the mating dance of the **bumblebee** with my car to my friend here.

How to get out of a fight when you are surrounded:

You know skunks?

Well, I was found by a family of skunks when I was a day old and they brought me up to be just like them. I can forage for plums on a moonless night and fire a toxic substance out of my bottom up to 50 feet that will burn your corneas and render you incapable of controlling your bowel movements for 48 hours!

How to get out of queuing to get into a club:

I'm the **toilet attendant**. It's my first day!

How to get out of cleaning the hamster cage:
I spoke to Bernard [or whatever the hamster is called] last night – we had a bit of a heart to heart – and he told me that he is learning to become a **Jedi master**. To do this, he needs to be in solitary confinement for three weeks to channel his thought processes and any disturbance to his cage would ruin his training. I can't do that to the little fella.

How to get out of kissing your boyfriend when he has a beard:
It's like **kissing a sheep** and I'm afraid I'll get the irresistible urge to herd you with my shepherd's crook.

How to get out of eating the meal that your partner has taken four hours to cook:
I'm doing a **sponsored fast**. Sorry I didn't tell you before; it slipped my mind – must be the lack of food making me forgetful.

120

How to get out of holding hands:
I went to the doctor today and have been told I have a **fungal infection** in my fingernails — apparently it's because I spend too much time dislodging wax from my ears with them. I don't even know when I'm doing it.

How to get out of giving away your last chocolate:
My grandfather was a miner and he always told me to leave the last piece for the **kelpies** for good luck. You are not a kelpie, so you can't have it.

How to get out of being designated driver on a trip to the pub:
What a **lovely conversation** I've had with that person over there. [Point to a mirror on the wall.]

How to get out of buying a birthday present:
After you said that Valentine's Day was a **cynical** marketing ploy, I didn't want to offend you by making a fuss on your birthday.

How to get out of giving up your seat on the bus:
I sprained my **groin** while rescuing a family of ducks from a drain – do forgive me, but I can barely stand.

How to get out of a drinking game with a mafia don:
I've been **teetotal** since 1983. I mistakenly ate a liqueur chocolate two Christmases ago and became so angry that I massacred my neighbours, or so I've been told – I remember nothing of the incident.

How to get out of playing Russian roulette:
Sorry, anything Russian makes me come out in hives. I think it was from that time when I wouldn't buy this manky bit of **lucky heather** from a babushka at Shepherd's Bush tube station. She must have put a hex on me.

How to get out of changing a lightbulb:
I ate **15 carrots** today; I do not need the light on.

How to get out of going to Slough: I hear that they emit a **dangerous** electrical frequency from their phone masts in Slough, due to the amount of text messages sent at any one time – it can cause swelling to the frontal lobe and lead to early **death**. Just think of the children!

How to get out of being roped in to trying a position from the Kama Sutra: I couldn't possibly without six months' training from an Indian master– that position takes **immense skill** you know!

How to get out of going on the Boxing Day walk:
Last time I went on a Boxing Day walk I got shot in the **arse**!

How to get out of going on a roller coaster:
I'll just be **sick** on your head now, shall I?

How to get out of saying '**I love you**':
You're all right, aren't you? [Pat them on the head and sneeze in their face.]